Saving Retirement NOW!

How Index Annuities Can Keep You From Losing Your Money

And

Provide an Guaranteed Income For The Rest of Your Life!

Market Gains, No Market Losses
Beat the Bank
Guaranteed Income

By:
Kenny Phillips

ISBN: 978-0-9842686-0-3

Alakazam Publishing, LLC
6182 NW 23rd St
Boca Raton, FL 33432

www.alakazampublishing.com
Sales@AlakazamPublishing.com

Table of Contents

Table of Contents

Introduction:

Is the Time Right for Index Annuities?

Have YOU lost enough money, yet?
If you just can't take it anymore, read on....

The past couple of years have been painful. Millions of people have lost their jobs and homes. We as a nation, rich and poor, have lost trillions in wealth and now question whether the promise of America is still there.

America Will Survive and Prosper!

I believe strongly that the promise of America is still strong, although hidden behind overzealous reporters and hype from our government. I further believe that we will emerge from this situation stronger and richer than we were when the mess began.

Now, while that's great for the youngsters out there, for those of us who are baby boomers or already retired, the rebuilding process may seem a little long and rough. In fact, it may seem <u>too</u> long and rough.

And that is what I want to tell you about today. If you are retired or are staring retirement squarely in the face, **<u>what do you do now</u>**, knowing that a recovery might be years in the making?

And how long will that recovery take? You see, the problem for most of us is that by the time this problem is over, we will be (or should have been) retired and living the easy life. That is not so much the case anymore.

A 'No Brainer'

I want to tell you about what I call a 'no brainer.' This is an idea that is so timely, so appropriate and so ideal, for lack of a better word, when you understand it you will say, "Of course, that makes perfect sense!"

No, I didn't make this up, nor is it new or based on the promise or projection of future growth. In fact, this idea is most needed when growth is lacking or when it's inconsistent, such as NOW!

Its time has come!

This idea has been around a long while, but for baby boomers or retirees, the people who are close to the end, people who cannot afford these constant market losses, suddenly this idea stands up and shouts, "Use me; helping to lower risk is what I was made for!"

Call me crazy perhaps, but read on and I think you may see the merit in my strategy.

I see a 'no brainer' as an investment that is:

- Less Risky
- Liquid
- Understandable
- Timely, in that it meets the desires/concerns of what people may want at that time

6

- Popular (it's not undiscovered or subject to discovery like a list of internet or gold mining stocks that are about to "explode!")
- It has been around for a while and has been well-tested
- It can handle large sums of money going into it

You already know that there is no such thing as a perfect investment every investment has qualities that make it imperfect, but sometimes, just sometimes the economic situation, our place in history, our leadership in Washington and other factors make one investment, become a very popular choice that gives people what they want, when they want it. I believe that may be what is happening now to indexed annuities.

Here are some examples of what I mean from the history books. Let's see if you remember any of them:

'No Brainers' of the Past

- Remember CDs when they used to pay 13% or more with FDIC or FSLIC insurance? Those were 'no brainers!' Who isn't happy that they invested in them?!

- How about "AAA/AAA" rated municipal bonds yielding as much as 14%? These where tax-free 'no brainers!' Looking back it was obvious they were a good deal and we knew it at the time.

- How about 15% low income tax credit housing? A huge winner! You put money in and the government gave it back to you in a few years via tax credits. This was so popular they sold out.

- How about stocks just after the 1987 crash! Another "no brainer!" That's why the market responded so quickly after the crash- people jumped on those low prices. (It may not be like that today, and you know why!)

- Also REITS during the stock market bubble in 1999 and 2000, yielding 12% in dividends or better. Many of them doubled even as the stock market fell

And the list goes on and on. You might have your own that seemed so obvious that you wondered why they were even offered for sale. I believe and I want to try to show to you that it may be such a time again.

Did you own any of those 'no brainers?' Probably yes, you did. Each of them met the qualities of what a 'no brainer' investment is and was.

These days are different though. The markets have taken a lot of losses from nearly all investments and the experts say the recovery may take 5 years or more. Some are comparing us to Japan, which was idle for 10 years. We hope that's not the case now.

The good news is that the experts can and have been wrong. After all- they didn't *predict* this mess, so who says they know how long it will last? Again of course, that's great for the younger investors but what a about seasoned investors with shorter time horizons?

What happens if we don't grow for 10 years; are you ready?

If we get into a period of no growth for 10 years, we had better have a plan to deal with it, and furthermore, if we do grow, be it next year or in the years to come, we had better have a plan to profit from that as well. Here's the good news: Index Annuities may help cover both bases! And at a time when we are so close to retirement we have to cover all bases.

Right Now There is basically a 0% Yield in Money Market Funds or Government Bonds

What are you to do when the money markets and CDs have nearly no yield at all, and what yield there is gets subjected to income tax?

If you don't invest you get nothing, and inflation takes away your purchasing power. Yet if you buy stocks instead, you might get hammered with more losses.

The stock market, which seems pretty low, is also more volatile that ever, which is confusing the experts and causing a lot of people to sit on the sidelines, perhaps for a long time. (Japan sat around doing nothing for 10 plus year after their real estate-based bubble!)

What are <u>you</u>, a prudent, sensible investor, to do now to preserve <u>your capital</u> and get it ready to help generate income for <u>your retirement</u>?

The answer for many, especially those who are willing to give up the possibility of really big gains in exchange for giving up the potential of additional big market losses, maybe an **<u>Index Annuity</u>**.

<u>An Index Annuity is NOT like an index mutual fund</u>.

9

Index Mutual Funds go UP with the markets and DOWN with them too.

An **Index Annuity** goes up with the markets but <u>not</u> down with them. It's not magic, and don't worry, it's not Bernie Madoff either.

Do you see why I think it maybe timely? Hey, if we were all 30 years old, this wouldn't make as much sense, but since I suspect you aren't, getting those market losses out of the equation maybe attractive. In fact, it's becoming a necessity for a lot of people I know, as they are losing sleep, arguing with their spouses and making other bad choices with their time and money in the face of this stressful economic situation.

Speaking of not being 30, let's talk about some adult things, one of the imperfect things about index annuities is that you can lose money with them- I know that sounds shocking but it's true. If you put the money in and want to take it back out before it's committed time there are surrender penalties like a certificate of deposit or other annuity products, or if you invest in an insurance company that goes under you may get back less money than you put it. Of course there are things that can help protect you from that happening, including picking a good company to invest in, and making sure you can wait to get your principal back until the surrender penalty is up.

But as we are speaking as adults we know that there is no perfect investment and there are costs and risks in everything. The one risk that index annuities take out of the equation is that daily change in your portfolio and the emotional rollercoaster that causes many people. Also index annuities offer a guaranteed income feature which I will go over soon and it the real reason I believe they are so very popular.

Maybe it's time for a little less greed and a little less emotion, and reduced worry, I believe that this is the calling of the indexed annuity.

It's no wonder that the alcohol stocks are doing OK in this market; there is a lot of "self medication" going on to combat the stress!

Does this sound WAY too good to be true???

It's not!

Keep reading and I will explain the nuts and bolts and show you how you may find the confidence to sleep at night again.

Imagine having an investment with:

- No management fees
- No current income taxes on earnings, pay the taxes when you take the money out
- No up-front sales loads
- No prospectus
- Reduced market risks such as market losses, currency fluctuations, manager changes, capital gain distributions or any of that stuff!

But more, how about guarantees that you will have an income based upon an amount far in excess of what you put in, even if the markets go down year after year.

What I am about to discuss is an example; for discussion purposes only, any contract you invest in will likely be different, and maybe even better, as these figures depend on when you invest, your age and how your specific investment is structured.

Imagine at age 70 you put in $100,000. At the end of ten years, if the stock market only goes down, never up, not even for a single day, you will be able to take an income of $8,881 a year guaranteed by the insurance company for the rest of your life.

Try to beat that with a CD, or with a stock, or some other types of investments. You can't, because none of those things offer these guarantees:

- The value of the account will not suffer from market losses, and

- A guaranteed income that is potentially in excess of what a CD is likely to earn in the immediate future. A quick question: How much money would you have to have in a CD at 2% to get income of $8,881 for the rest of your life? I think that number is $444,000. But a CD doesn't even have a guarantee that long. The beauty of an Index Annuity is that it guarantees to pay that income; the simple explanation for how they can afford to do this is in this book.

- You can turn it in and get your money back (subject to surrender charge if you turn it in early, of course) and go elsewhere if you find a better deal.

Did I mention that there is no prospectus required like with a security? What does that tell you? It tells me that Index

Annuities are simple, guaranteed by the insurance companies that issue them, and not subject to a lot of the games that they play on Wall Street. That's what a prospectus does, by the way; it tells you in advance about all the things that can go wrong and all the conflicts of interest. That's not needed here.

Do you see how this could benefit you at a time when all of us are worried to death about our retirements and where that cash flow is going to come from? This potentially helps protect us from market declines and also helps provide guarantees on that income that we will need at retirement.

Like CDs and municipal bonds in the early 80's, and stocks in the late 80's and on and on- this is the 'no brainer' for 2009.

Remember what a 'no brainer' is? Let's review....

- Less Risk: YES! These annuities are issued by the biggest insurance companies in the world.

- Liquid: YES! They have cash value and can be surrendered at any time; like CDs they will have penalties for early surrender and you might lose money but they are liquid.

- Understandable: YES! You have a contract, with a company you choose that specifies what the minimum earnings are and how they are calculated.

- Timely: YES! I think right now people may want something that will not lose money, can perhaps make money, and even if the markets don't recover and has the ability to yield a healthy income.

- <u>Popular</u>: YES! These things are incredibly popular!

- It has been around for a while: YES! These have been around since 1995 and the money in them has been growing quickly, especially as in the past few years they have gotten a lot better terms and appear to be a better deal (in my opinion) than the first ones.

- It can handle large sums of money going into it: YES! No problem, the insurance companies can issue lots of these.

The companies that are issuing these contracts are seeing more business than they ever have, some with growth rates approaching 50% a year, while inflows into many other investments are shrinking at incredible rates, and it's no wonder why.

No More Mistakes

For a lot of people who are getting tired of the losses or are getting close to retirement and can't afford to make any more mistakes, this is the idea that will allow them to truly understand what their minimum retirement income will be, understand when it will be available, and will let them sleep at night. (And sleep really well, too!)

I want to share with you two quick stories. One story is about pigs and the other is about two brothers.
First the brothers…

This is a true story; I was told this story recently at a conference I attended. This was a conference of professionals, like me, who gathered to discuss the status of things and the best things to do with our money and that of our clients that has been entrusted to us. It shines a light on how much fear and anger is out there.

A Story of Two Brothers, Bob and Ed

Two brothers, Bob and Ed, always competed with each other, and the older of the two, Bob, made it a point to be bigger and better than his younger brother, Ed. Each Thanksgiving the families switched the home they celebrated in; one year it was Bob's home and the next year it was Ed's home.

This story takes place last Thanksgiving, when the family was gathered at Bob's home.

While both brothers are investors, Bob was notorious for bragging about how big his portfolio had become, always making more than everybody else in the room.

Ed, the younger of the two, was not as aggressive with his money and always took a more moderate course. Early in 2008, a very good friend of his showed him Index Annuities and he switched a large portion of his Rollover IRA into them. Ed didn't show Bob what he had done, as he didn't want the predictable laughter and comments about his lack of guts.

During the course of the afternoon while the meal was being prepared, Bob (the aggressive one) was bragging again, this time not about his gains but about how much money he had lost due to the global economic meltdown.

Bob went on an on endlessly about the hammering that he was taking in the markets, looking down 20% on that account, 40% on another, and so forth.

During this tirade, Ed (the conservative one) kept his mouth tightly shut, despite being prodded many times by Bob, who would ask, "How are you doing with your stuff?"

Eventually Bob couldn't take not knowing anymore, and as the dirty plates were being cleared off the table, he shouted at his brother, Ed, to tell him what he was up to. With his fist clenched and probably his very manhood and virility at stake, Bob grabbed Ed by the shirt and looked him in the eye and said, "I have to know. Tell me what you are doing. How much money have you lost?"

(Remember- this is a true story!)

Ed simply said, "None."

Bob was notably shocked and asked again. When Ed answered that he had taken steps to prevent any losses, Bob called Ed a liar and pressed him over and over again about how he could not have lost "ANY" money.

After all, Bob was invested in indexes too, and indexes had gone down; how could Ed not have lost money?

Ed said it was not an index fund he was invested in, but an Index Annuity, which allowed that not only would he not lose when the market goes down, but he would profit when the index went up. Wisely, Ed didn't mention the guaranteed income part of the deal.

During dessert Bob starting hitting on the wine really hard and mumbling under his breath about how that wasn't possible, and how he has the best people working for him and yet, he still lost money.

He glared at Ed, and the rest of the family could see the wheels turning in his head as he tried to understand how that was even possible.

Bob was frustrated beyond words. First, because his investment strategy was not the best there was, and secondly, because his younger brother, his junior in most things, had successfully found out about something that saved him all that money, the frustration and the sleepless nights. That really bugged him.

The brothers did not come to blows that day but I am told it was close.

In the years to come, Bob, the aggressive one, may overtake the conservative Ed in his investment returns, but he will have to do it starting from lower levels due to the losses he suffered before and after this past Thanksgiving.

It seems mathematically that it's much easier to gain in your accounts if you don't start with a 40% loss of the principal. I guess everyone knows that now!

As I write this, Ed's Index Annuities are not down in value at all, and in fact have reset so that if the market goes up from these low levels he will profit. Life is good for Ed.
Which one of these brothers would you want to be like, investment-wise?

I am sure that Bob is sweating the thought of next Thanksgiving, to be held at Ed's house. Will the market recover so that he can overcome the losses and get ahead of Ed? Or will he once again be in the backseat?

It may be a travel agent that wins, as Bob may decide to take his side of the family on a cruise in order to avoid the frustration and embarrassment of another family Thanksgiving!

Here's the PIG story!

This brings me to the second story. It's a one liner and fits today's times.

It goes like this, "When the trough gets empty, the pigs get mean."

It means of course that when pigs are feeding at a trough and the food runs low, the big pigs push the little pigs out of the way and snort at each other.

They get mean.

This is going on right now in the financial services industry.

The people have been taking their money out of the stock market, billions coming out, and Index Annuities are seeing record amounts of money coming in, with more business than some of the companies can handle.

This is making the big pigs (other investments) upset with the Index Annuity people, as when that money leaves those other investments, it stops paying the managers, the investment companies and all those people on Wall Street the big fees. You see, the Index Annuities don't have those big fees.

Who do you think wins on this deal?

THE LESSON HERE:

Don't expect your "Big Pig" (your investment broker) to be too happy about discussing an Index Annuity.

To be clear, there is no such thing as a *perfect* investment. I believe that's true. However occasionally, though not often, we get the opportunity for what I like to call a 'no brainer.' I believe this maybe one of those times!

The level of interest rates on government bonds, the stock market crash, the statements from the government that they will keep interest rates low quite some time, the global economic slump- these things all combine in such a way that I believe Index Annuities, if properly owned and structured, are possibility what I like to call a 'no brainer' *at this point in time*.

That's why I put this book together!

Years ago before you bought your first investments, CD or stock, you had to learn about them- how they worked, what the risks were, what the terms meant and so forth, right?

That is why I have put together this book- to help you through that process. These are pretty simple things, but like anything else, you will want to understand how they do what they do, what the tradeoffs are, who stands behind them, and so forth. The more you know, the better decisions you will make, and the more sleep you might get once you make an educated investment. I am not trying to make you an expert, just a well-informed consumer.

I hope you will see the wisdom and opportunity that I see in investing in Index Annuities in these rough economic times. This idea seems as close to perfect as they come. Please use this as a resource to help you see if Index Annuities can help you sleep better at night!

In the coming pages I will discuss the workings of Index Annuities that you must know to make them work for you. These are not hard to understand or use, as you can tell by the small size of this book. Be comforted by such a small sized instruction book, but don't judge it by its size; the following pages are full of important information and that all-important checklist to go over with your agent to be sure you 'got it!'

Notice

Throughout this book I will be discussing various terms and conditions and characteristics of variable and Index Annuities. This business is getting more competitive nearly every day so the terms and examples that I use are intended to be general in nature. You need to discuss with a competent agent the specific characteristics of the contract that you are investing in and not rely on the general educational discussions here in this book.

In these matters consult with legal tax and financial planning counsel to determine the correct ownership and beneficiary provisions as well as planning any tax or creditor preservation strategy.

Chapter 1

What is an Index Annuity?

If you look up the word annuity in the dictionary it will tell you that an annuity is a stream of payments, lasting for a certain period of time or perhaps until the end of someone's life. An Index Annuity may or may not turn into a stream of payments; that is the choice of the owner, and I will cover that shortly.

When we talk about annuities there are fixed annuities and variable annuities. An Index Annuity is a FIXED annuity, which means that the value of the account does <u>not</u> decrease as a result of changes in the stock market. A fixed annuity pays a stated rate of interest (like 5%) and the balance in the annuity does not change (it's fixed) once the interest has been paid. A Fixed <u>Index</u> Annuity uses the change in a stock market index, such as the Dow Jones 30 Industrials, to determine how much interest you are paid, and once the interest is paid, the value of your account does not go down, even if the Dow Jones does.

That's the really neat thing about an Index Annuity is how the interest that is paid to you is computed. If you invest and the stock market goes up, so then does the value of the index annuity. But it the market goes down your value doesn't. I will cover more of how this happens in Chapter 2.

If the market goes down you will earn little or no interest; some contracts promise to pay you a little interest even if the market goes down.

> Example: For the sake of our discussion let's say that the contract you select pays nothing if the stock market (as measured by the index you select) goes down. But it the stock market goes up, you get paid interest based on how much it goes up. Suppose the

indexes that the company offers, and that you select, go up by 10% during the course of the year. If your contract provides that you have a 100% participation rate then your annuity will earn interest of 10% for that year. That's great!

Instead let's suppose that the stock market goes down 10% for the year and you have a 100% participation rate. You would earn… 0% interest, and thereby not lose any value due to the market losses. That's great too! You can't put a dollar figure on the confidence you can have in knowing your investments are preserved and aren't getting hammered by the markets.

It's a Contract

An Index Annuity is a contract between you, the investor (usually called the owner), and an insurance company. You don't get to negotiate the contract as you might with a contract for purchase or sale of your home; the insurance company draws it up, submits it to the state you live in for approval, and once approved, offers it for sale, generally through qualified agents in your state.

So you, or your agent, get to shop around and choose between the various offerings of the insurance companies that are licensed to do business in your state of residence.

You can compare the offerings, review the financial strengths of the companies and then decide which one or more (you may want to spread your investment among different companies) you might invest in.

Different insurance companies offer different types of Index Annuities, some don't offer any, and some specialize in this type of product. Your favorite insurance company may or may not be in this marketplace.

At the end of each year, you will get a statement showing the change in the index and how your interest is calculated. The next year begins and you start again. Usually you are offered the chance to change the index you want to use to compute your interest on (that's very handy) and, and this is important, any interest that you earned due to market gains (that's the way you earn interest) can never be lost later due to subsequent market declines.

This feature of not giving back last year's gains is one that a lot of people appreciate these days; in 2008 and 2009 many people gave back stock market gains that it took them years to build up. They thought the money was theirs and then the markets took it back. Not so with an Index Annuity!

As time goes by the value of your annuity should go up in value as the markets go up. You then have a choice about how to get your money out of the contract. (See Chapter 10)

Variable Annuities vs. Index Annuities

Remember that an Index Annuity is a type of fixed annuity. A variable annuity is an annuity contract too, but its value is determined by summing up the investments that it owns so if the market goes down, the value of the variable annuity goes down. Not so with a Fixed Index Annuity. So if, in the above example, the market went down 10% and the variable annuity was invested in the same index, then it would lose 10% in value, plus any fees and such that are being charged to the investment accounts within the annuity.

A variable annuity is invested in sub accounts (like mutual funds), and each one of those is run by managers and fund companies (some of whom are excellent investment managers).

They have expenses and do the best they can. There is no guarantee that they will match the markets or beat them, or that the markets will do better than them. The managers of the sub accounts have to overcome their fees and costs before they can give you positive returns. An Index Annuity has none of that- no fees or costs of management. You will know at the beginning of the year what you will get at the end (when you know what the index does for the year). There are no surprises and no excuses.

Variable annuities are very powerful tools, and in a very good year when the markets are soaring, variable annuities will outperform Index Annuities.

But in a market that looks weak or where people are scared and want to avoid any losses in value, an Index Annuity is usually more popular for obvious reasons, being that it doesn't go down in value if the market does. Variable annuities can lose not only this year's gains but last year's as well, so 5 years of good performance can go away in one bad year (this just happened). Index Annuities reset each year so that any gains made last year are retained.

Should You Choose Variable or Fixed Index Annuities?

Right now many people are moving toward Index Annuities to get away from this risk of loss of principal, as these losses in the markets have been pretty severe lately. However, if you have a short life expectancy, such as if you are not in good health, you might want to consider a variable annuity instead. Variable annuities (remember- they go up and down) usually have a feature that promises to pay you back your total investment if and when you DIE. If you know that is likely in the short run, go for the possible higher returns that variable annuities might yield, because your family can count on getting your money back when your time is up.

For example, if you have end-stage cancer, and the doctors say you have less than a year to live, you might invest in a variable annuity and choose very aggressive sub accounts to put the money in. The investments would probably make or lose a lot of money in the next year. If they make money your family will keep the profits; however, if the investments lose money, then when you die your family will get all of your investment back because of that guarantee in the variable annuity that says that upon death you will get your original investment back as a minimum.

So if the investments go up, you win; if they go down, you (your heirs) get it all back with no loss. It's a great strategy except for the dying part.

Alternatively, an index annuity promises never to let the account value go down, but on the other hand, if the market goes up 40% you might not get all of that profit. How much you get is based on the insurance company you decide on, the indexes they offer and you choose, the participation rates and so forth. That's part of the trade-off.

So if you are going to be around for a while, an Index Annuity may be the desirable choice; it gets a little less of the upside, but none of the losses. See your agent or advisor for more guidance on using this type of investment to help preserve your wealth.

One More Subtle but Important Difference…

There is one more big difference between variable annuities and Index Annuities that comes into play if you want to get your money out of the contract.

An Index Annuity is guaranteed not to go down in value because of the markets, so if another investment comes along, one that you think is better and would rather invest in, you will be able to get access to all the money you put in, as well as whatever gains have been credited, less any surrender penalties or costs of additional riders you chose and re-invest it. With a variable contract, the account value may have gone down, so you might only get back a fraction of what you put in; that is, unless you die.

Some variable annuities offer riders which guarantee that after, say, 7 years your account will not be worth less than what you put in. It sounds like an Index Annuity. They do that by restricting how you invest the money in the account, so you are prohibited from making investments that can really generate a lot of profit. Further, with a variable annuity you might have 6 really good years and in that 7th year, lose a portion, perhaps large or perhaps small amount of value. This just happened to a lot of people in 2008.

If you instead have six good years with an Index Annuity and the 7th is very bad, you get to keep all the interest (gains) from the first six and would likely come out ahead of the variable contract, perhaps far ahead.

In the end, not going down in value when the stock market does can be a great advantage. These subtle sounding differences are really quite significant in volatile markets and will potentially help save the day and the retirement for some people.

A variable annuity also usually has a death benefit which pays you back what you put in and sometimes even more (usually for an extra cost) when you die, but an index annuity doesn't need to do that because the markets can't force the value of it down.

Riders

An important concept here is that a lot of these annuities have (or can have) special riders that include a guarantee to pay income even if the contract didn't earn it. Or, there might be a rider available which increases the amount you can take out for nursing home or home health care needs. This is a very important point and not to be overlooked.

A rider, by the way, is a supplement to the contract. It, too, is written by the company. It adds additional benefits, and usually costs as well, to the contract. Typically in Index Annuities the only costs you will see are due to the riders you add on. Yet even though they add extra costs they can add some significant benefits. We'll talk more about riders in Chapter 3.

Intangible Benefits

Let's face it- these have been some rough times lately. No American family is untouched by the loss of value and jobs, and the anger and frustration and denial that come with events of the magnitude we have seen. But when you own Index Annuities, the lack of apprehension that you may feel when you turn on the news channels to hear the day's financial news may be like a wonderful dessert at the end of a fine meal.

By investing in Index Annuities you can't think about what the markets did "today", because only the performance over a longer period of time will count. You won't have to worry about all those things that make the market move short term-interest rates, unemployment rates, trade deficits, government deficits, corruption on Wall Street, politicians trying to sound like economists and on and on. The guarantees of the income benefit will give you more confidence in your ability to survive retirement tomorrow, and that may allow you to live a better, less stressful and more productive life today. Please consider this intangible benefit in your decision making model; a life with less panic and anxiety is good for you, your health and your family!

Summary

An Index Annuity is a contract, between you and an insurance company of your choosing, that allows you to be paid interest when the market indexes you pick go up, but not lose any interest (value) once the interest has been paid, even if the market falls. The insurance company may have riders (usually a small extra cost) that amplify the amount of income you can take out even if the market never goes up at all, as well as additional riders and options you can choose. Each company is different and the business is evolving and getting more competitive all the time!

The differences between Index Annuities and variable annuities are pretty significant and need to be understood. Both are powerful vehicles that try to deliver to people the power of the stock market in different ways and to different degrees.

Chapter 2

How Do Index Annuities Work?

You're likely starting to wonder, "If I earn interest when the market goes up, but don't lose when it goes down, how is that possible? What's the catch?"

As an <u>owner</u> of an Index Annuity you don't need to know all the details of how they work; you really only need to have faith in your insurance company to live up to its promises. This is because the guarantees from the insurance company on the base policy, as well as the riders, override the busy nuts and bolts that make it all work. We'll talk more about guarantees later.

As an <u>investor</u> though, you may want to know how things work so you can evaluate whether it's a good deal, truly understand what is happening with your money, and make informed decisions regarding your investments. So I'm going to share with you the nuts and bolts of how Index Annuities work. (If Bernie Madoff's investors had demanded this kind of information maybe they would still have their money!)

Relax- there will NOT be a test!

In a typical Index Annuity you give the insurance company a sum of money, say $100,000, and the company guarantees you that at the end of the term your account value will not go down because of market changes, and will in fact go up via the crediting of interest to the contract if your indexes go up in value. In Chapter 7 we will talk more about the indexes you can choose.

Let's take a look at how that works:

The company takes your $100,000 and pays from it whatever premium tax is due to the state you live in. In Florida, for instance, the state collects a tax on each premium and uses it to build our fire stations in much of the state.

With the remaining money the company buys some zero coupon bonds that will mature when the contract is up. Let's say that those bonds cost $85,000. These bonds will mature at $100,000 and so your principal is guaranteed by the insurance company, but it further backed up by its investment in the bonds.

This leaves the insurance company with about $15,000 plus or minus left over. Out of that money the company does several things. First, it pays its necessary operating expenses, including a commission to your agent, its overhead, its legal costs, and of course it maintains an element for its profit as well.

The largest share of that money goes to buy a contract with someone else that promises to pay the company a profit if the index goes up. These are called "call options." Basically it's a bet that pays off if the index goes up and becomes worthless if it goes down.

If the index goes up, the company uses the profit from the call to pay you your percentage of that gain. If it doesn't go up or if it goes down, the company has the $85,000 in bonds that mature at $100,000 when the term of your contract is up. This is also why having an early withdraw penalty is important, as the company needs time for that bond to grow in value from $85,000 to $100,000. That $100,000 will be used to pay you back your investment if the stock market does nothing but go down.

The term of your contract is the amount of time until the contract is liquid and you can withdraw all the money you put in plus the interest that has been credited without any penalty. When its' time to measure the interest (growth) you have earned, the change in the index is measured and your contract is credited the interest you have earned. This will come from the appreciation of the "call" or the bet that was placed.

It's actually a pretty simple transaction but does take some skill to balance out the various numbers; hence, the guarantee of the insurance company to deliver the results without showing you the moving parts underneath makes Index Annuities really simple and easy to own and understand.

Each time the contract is measured, the term is reduced and the various factors change. When interest is credited to the contract it is taken away from the call and used to purchase more bonds.

If the market goes down a lot the index will go down too, and so will the call option that the company bought, but that doesn't matter. Your investment is backed not only by the insurance company guarantees (See Chapter 8), which is the really important thing, but also by its ownership of the zero coupon bonds which will come due at the same $100,000 you put in.

How Do the Riders Work?

If you elect to add on any riders, such as one to give you a greater income than the contract may otherwise allow (and which I think is probably a must in today's uncertain times), or one that might provide other benefits, the cost of the rider comes out of the contract and is paid to the insurance company. They calculate the risk they are taking in making that promise to you, the use of their capital and so forth, and come up with the cost. It's one of the great things that they can do, by using their ability to make long term promises. (More about riders in Chapter 3)

That is how an Index Annuity works; it's pretty simple really. A question that often comes up is: If it's so simple and easy to do, why don't I just do it myself and avoid the costs of the insurance company?

Here's why you might not want to do it without them:

- The insurance company has the scale size and know-how to do this cheaply.

- They have the guarantee and net worth to use to back stop all the details, so you as a policy holder don't have to worry when a call expires or when those bonds mature and what it will cost them to replace the call or the bonds for the next go 'round. You as a policy holder simply have the guarantee of the insurance company to deliver to you an exact result.

- The insurance company, via its contract, can allow you to defer taxes, something you could not do on your own. Because you purchase an annuity contract, you (according to the IRS) don't have to pay income taxes on the profits until you take out the money. This can be a terrific benefit; if you don't need to spend the money, you don't have to withdraw it and so you, won't have to pay taxes on it, until you take it out.

- The insurance company, by issuing a contract in your state, may make your investment such that it is not subject to creditors. This is because your state's laws that may exempt annuities from the claims of most creditors.

And if that wasn't enough, here is….

The Big One:

There is no way that you as an individual can buy that guarantee to provide you with the cash flow I spoke of earlier. These days, prices of almost all assets are falling. So a promise from one of the largest insurance companies in the world to provide an income for life that is greater that most anything you could likely earn on the money yourself is a strong strategy to the retirement problem. That problem being, or course, how are you going to live and survive financially during your retirement years?!

For Example:

Remember in the introduction my example of the 70 year-old putting in $100,000 and being guaranteed a $8,881 a year cash flow starting 10 years later? This was guaranteed even if the stock market went down every year. There is no other financial instrument that I am aware of that individuals can buy that will provide such a guarantee.

If you invest $100,000 in a CD at 2% and let it compound for 10 years you will have, net of a 15% tax rate, a total of $120,000. You would need to earn an interest rate of 13% for life to earn the cash flow provided by the Index Annuity in this example.

With today's 2% interest rates, someone would have to have $444,000 invested in Certificates of Deposit to earn $8,881 a year. Index Annuity contracts have guarantees that may provide that cash flow for life. I believe that guarantees like this may keep those people who take advantage of Index Annuities from having to eat dog food in their retirement years!

Switching Indexes

Most Index Annuities have to have at least one moving part, and -here's the good news- it's not the declining value of your money!

You don't buy an Index Annuity for a one year period, and yet each year you get a chance to switch the index and/or crediting method and earn money in other ways. This is a great feature and is part of the improvements that the industry has been making over the past 4 years.

Let me share with you a complexity that comes with giving you this flexibility. At the start of the contract, (remember the $100,000 I spoke of earlier?) there is a fixed amount of money to split up between the various needs, including overhead, costs of acquisition, cost of bonds, and cost of the call to give you your interest. We used the Dow Jones Index in our previous discussion.

What happens when, a year later, you want to switch indexes but all the prices have changed? Some have gone up, and some have gone down.

In order to allow the whole thing to work, the company can change some terms on what they can pay you (it goes both ways more or less) depending on what it needs to buy calls.

The company protects itself and you by putting caps (the highest you can earn) or spreads (it takes so much off the top) to allow all the math to work out right.

The company cannot ask you for more money if the calls it has to buy go up in cost or because you want to switch the index you want to use to calculate your interest to another one. Instead it compensates by moving some of the other factors around.

Chapter 3

Options: Riders and Bonuses

In this chapter let's talk about the extras, those riders I have spoken of that can add value to the contract, especially in tough financial times, and bonuses.

As I have mentioned before, each company is different and offers many different options, and the list is changing often. My goal here is to acquaint you with a few general ones, so that when you run across variations on them it will be easier to understand what they mean.

Guaranteed Income Riders

A rider like this can allow you to take a lot more money out of an Index Annuity than it has in it, and will allow you to continue to do so for life. That is a pretty impressive accomplishment, and may well be a lifesaver for many people over the next 30 years or so.

As the stock market has reduced the value of all of our IRAs and 401(k)s and other retirement plans, we are worried about where the income will come from that we will need to supplement Social Security benefits. I suggest that it might very well come from these types of riders.

They work mostly like this: You put a sum of money into the annuity and every year, whether it grows or not, the company credits your "income account" for a sum of money. Now, this isn't money you can take out that year, it's just a running balance that will be used later to compute an income stream that the company will guarantee for life.

The longer the contract is in force, the more it adds up. Any distributions from the contract might reduce it, depending on the details in your particular contract. Hence, the income rider in a market that is not going up or in a market that is going down may be priceless.

An income rider on your contract during a market that is going up each year may not have much value, as your contract value will be more than the total of your contributions and the income rider credits.

The point of the rider then is to guarantee a good cash flow from the contract if stocks go up or down, but also to give you the confidence that you can have a suitable retirement income. It's a 'sleep at night' type of assurance.

Should you exercise the rider, your income begins right away, based usually on your age, and the total in the income rider formula multiplied by a percentage. The result of this is the annual amount of cash you can take out for life.

In the example I used in the introduction, $100,000 goes in for a 70 year-old, and the income rider alone will, ten years later, pay out $8,884 or so per year for life. I think that's pretty good and can help a lot of people.

The money you take out reduces your account balance of course, as does the cost of the rider; this is an add-on and not part of the basic contract.

Over time, assuming the markets never go up, your annuity may be emptied of value as you receive your annual income payments, but you will continue to get the income off the rider just as before, with the insurance company coming out of pocket for your income for the rest of your life. Nobody actually wants the markets to stay in decline, but this is a handy bit of reassurance "just in case."

It's not available anywhere else, than from annuity contracts.

The more likely scenario is that your contract goes up some years because the market does, while it doesn't go down in other years when the market does (because market losses can't make it go down), and by the time you need it, it should, on its own or in conjunction with the rider, give you an income for as long as you need it, and the remaining money will subsequently be left to your family after your death.

Death Benefit Riders

Many companies offer death benefit riders, and these can be profitable. They offer an additional payout of usually 25% of the contract or of the gains in the contract.

If you are ill you might consider such a rider, even though there is an additional cost to it which varies from contract to contract. Usually it must be taken out at the inception of the contract.

Early Surrender Riders

Some companies offer riders that allow you to surrender your contract early, usually for a payout of its value over a short period of time. If you think you will need such a thing, you might consider it. If there is a cost for it you might also consider splitting your investment into two contracts; one with the rider and one without, so as to save some costs.

Nursing Home and Hospital Riders

These riders may allow you to get access to some or all of your money without any contractual penalty if you end up in a nursing home or hospital.

The industry is working hard to come up with more creative features and benefits to give more people more options. When you run across something new, email us at questions@alakazampublishing.com and let us know.

Bonuses

Many of the Index Annuity contracts today will give you a bonus for investing. It might be 5% on top of what you put in, or 10%, or even upwards of 25%. Some contracts may allow you add money in later years and get an additional bonus. If properly done this can be used to potentially increase your yield.

Bonuses are wonderful but if you surrender the contract early they will take some or all of it back, in addition to the surrender penalty. Some agents will describe the contract as one where they give you a 10% bonus to sign up and there is a surrender charge of 10% for the first "x" number of years, thereby leading you to believe that the bonus will take care of the surrender charge. Not so; they will take back the bonus (or a part of it) and charge the surrender penalty as well.

Also, remember the old adage: "There is no such thing as a free lunch." And remember also, that all the moving parts in an Index Annuity are related. What this boils down to is don't focus solely on whatever bonus may be offered.

If the contract you have selected, based upon the strength of the company, the value to you of the indexes, and the methods of calculating interest, also has a bonus (it probably will) then yes, you should take it. What's important, in my opinion is not to buy a contract because of it's bonus. Please don't invest with a weaker company just because it has a bigger bonus or some other teaser feature. A bonus is just a piece of the pie.

The bonus feature started out years ago to allow people to get out of other contracts while still in their surrender penalty period; the bonus from the new contract would make up the difference.

Nowadays, due to the more competitive contracts and with income riders and other such things which tend to keep contracts from being surrendered, the business of moving Index Annuities around has slowed quite a bit. I think that is a good thing.

A Word of Advice:

Index Annuities may offer a lot of extras, but it's not about investing in the Index Annuity with the best deal up front. A lot of the pieces, including bonuses, surrender charges (which we'll talk about in Chapter 10), rider charges, the length of time the surrender penalty lasts, and so forth, are interrelated. By focusing on just one aspect of the annuity you might fall into a trap; instead look at each Index Annuity as a whole, especially considering the company that stands behind it.

Chapter 4

What Rate of Return Can I Expect?

This is always one of the best questions that I get. Index Annuities are for the risk-averse, not the greedy. While it is surely possible for an Index Annuity to generate some returns equal to those of other investments or better, it is not wise to invest in them for in the hopes of that specific result. If you want a return of 20% a year on your money, go get some other investments funds and take on the downside risk. Oh, and good luck!

As for putting a number on a return, I will say this (and I will ask, again, any greedy people who want to take a lot of risk and relive the past couple of year to please stop reading here and just go buy some stocks):

1) You will not lose money due to the stock market going down. That might be a pleasant change from your current investments, even money markets, which after taxes come pretty close to a zero net return. In that regard, in a down market these might equal money market funds.

2) If you choose an Index Annuity that has a guaranteed minimum return, say 4%, then you will be credited with a minimum of 4% interest; that beats most CDs, all money markets, most bond funds and just about all stocks and many other investments over the past couple of years.

3) Beyond not losing, and getting a minimum return if your index goes up, you will get more, simply based on the

math. There will be no mismanagement or poor excuses; you can do the math too, to figure out what you will get. Additionally, Index Annuities can do the following for you:

- Add some consistency to your returns
- Help defer and manage your taxes
- Help you avoid creditors
- Guarantee an income off the investment for your retirement

But please, don't ever count on Index Annuities to do the following for you:

Beat the markets-You will not get to brag about how you are doing better than the markets, UNLESS the markets go down (again) or up less than your guaranteed minimum interest rate, if you select that option.

Make you rich- It is very unlikely that an index annuity will take your $100,000 IRA and turn it into millions and millions of dollars. Perhaps it will eventually turn into a million if you give it enough time to compound, but certainly not in the short term.

Make you look as smart as Warren Buffett- That is, unless when the market goes down; then you may very well beat him!

What will I earn, exactly?

I would like to give you a fast number about exactly what you will earn on your Index Annuity but that's impossible.

What is important, if you can afford to leave your money in the index annuity for a while, is to look at whatever guaranteed income riders are available. Your bank or broker doesn't have "guaranteed income riders" unless they are selling annuities.

As we age and get closer to retirement, it becomes less about how much our money can grow each month or year and more about what it can provide for us in the way of cash flow and guarantees. This is where Index Annuities shine! And that's why at this point in time and for a long while, they may be a no brainier!

Who is best suited to invest in Index Annuities?

The people best suited to invest to in Index Annuities are those who want stability in their financial lives, (or more likely- those who want stability to return to their lives!) These people are concerned about their retirement, particularly their income at retirement, and want to do everything they can to maximize what they can get their hands on for the remainder of their life.

These people will have a long term perspective, not want to trade or change their investment very often, and will appreciate the consistency of having investments that go up or stay the same each year, but that don't go down because of market action.

The ideal Index Annuity investor is not greedy, nor do they think they have to be in the hottest investments out there (that's really the same thing). They will be the people who do not play "keeping up with the Joneses."

They are long-term investors who are saving toward a retirement or other goal which will require money, and a lot of it, to accomplish, and want guarantees on some of their investments that will help them reach that goal.

They will understand that in order to avoid market losses and perhaps be guaranteed a minimum rate of interest, they will give up some of the upside of investing in the stock market, and they will be happy to make that trade-off.

What they are after is stability, predictability, and strength, with perhaps guarantees thrown in just in case the markets don't do well for a very long time.

These people may have always been this way or may just be learning to be conservative. While they might be of any age, more likely they have a little grey in their hair, earned from experience, and have a desire not to repeat the near-death experience of recent market crashes.

If you are like that, or want to be, maybe Index Annuities are a good fit for some of your investments.

Is there anyone who should avoid index annuities?

People not suited to investing in Index Annuities might include:

1) Those who want to trade and move things around all the time. It's great that they want to be active, but an Index Annuity is not designed to be moved around other than once a year (usually), so frequent traders and those who change their minds often may feel trapped.

2) Those who are definitely going to be in higher tax brackets during their retirement years, such as those

expecting a very large inheritance. Such people may not be concerned about avoiding market declines and they may be in very high tax brackets, both then and now. Hence, the tax deferral is not so valuable to them. (Other benefits may still create enough value to make Index Annuities a smart move for them anyway!)

3) Those who have their money and investments held in partnerships or corporations. Those types of entities can't take advantage of the tax deferral aspects in Index Annuities. IRAs are ok though.

4) Those who need income from all of their investments right away; they may still be good investors for Index Annuities but that aspect should be carefully discussed with their agent.

5) People with personalities (like "Bob" in the introduction) who need to be fed with extremes. Index Annuities will not deliver for them at all, but for those like Bob's brother Ed, Index Annuities will probably work splendidly.

6) Those who feel they need FDIC insurance. Annuities are not FDIC insured, so if for some reason you need that particular safety net, an annuity of any sort may not be suitable. But, many people believe that annuity companies may be stronger that the FDIC, especially in these troubled times. It's hard for an insurance company that issues Index Annuities to have a run on it, simply by the nature of the longer term nature of the contract and the securities they typically buy to back them up. (See Chapter 2 regarding the contract and securities, and Chapter 8 for more information on guarantees.)

7) Those under age 59 ½. Since the distributions from an annuity contract that come from earnings are subject to a 10% penalty if taken before age 59 ½, people under that age should consider that when making their decision. Of course, if they have IRA money, which is subject to the same basic rules, an Index Annuity may be a good fit.

An Answer for the Risk-Averse Saver*

According to a study performed by DALBAR, Inc. (Quantitative Analysis of Investor Behavior, 1994), the **10-year performance of the Standard & Poor's 500 equity index between January 1984 and September 1993 was 293%**. Yet during the same period, the <u>average equity mutual fund investor made **only 70%.**</u>

The reason for the difference was this: In order to realize the 293% return, an investor had to "buy and hold" over the entire 10-year period. Unfortunately, many investors do not buy and hold. When the market goes down, they take their money out, hoping to avoid further losses.

While their money is out, they miss many of the market's upswings. This behavior occurs because of risk-aversion. In trying to avoid losses, risk-averse financial consumers may actually prevent themselves from realizing the gains they seek. Index Annuities allow risk-averse savers the opportunity to earn a rate of interest linked to equity performance, without fearing loss of principal due to market fluctuations, as long as they hold their Index Annuities to term. The Term of an index annuity will range from 5 to 25 years, with most about 10 years.

Index Annuities owners need not withdraw their money from their policies during market downturns for fear of incurring losses – they can feel reassured by the fixed annuity's minimum guarantees. They can keep their money in the policy until the markets turn back up, at which point they stand to earn potentially higher rates of interest linked to increases in the equity index.

*quoted from "Understanding Index Annuities" by Crump Insurance Services 02/08, emphasis added

Chapter 5

How is My Profit (Interest) Calculated?

Your growth in the contract will be paid by paying (they call it crediting) you with interest. This amount may be a minimum, perhaps zero or a higher number, depending on the method you select.

You may have an option of getting minimum interest rate. As I write this, some contracts carry a minimum of 4%, which is a lot higher than most bank CDs right now.

If you select a minimum rate then the other terms of the transaction may be changed. You will likely get less of the market upside, or there'll be a cap on how much additional interest you will earn if the markets go up.

There is no free lunch, but in the area of Index Annuities you may like the selections that are offered on this buffet of preservation!

You can earn more of course, than the minimum interest rate and that amount is based upon three things:

1) The index you select, you will get choices such as the Dow Jones 30 Industrials, S&P 500, and a variety of other internationally known and independently calculated indexes)

2) The participation rate of that index, limited by the spreads and caps (I will explain further on)

3) The crediting method

As we move through this terminology remember that you can never earn less that the minimum guarantee on your contract, and if you have chosen a contract with a minimum guarantee, you can never earn less than zero. This means of course, that market declines simply cannot cost you money.

I will use the Dow Jones 30 industrial average, or the "Dow," as the index for the examples that follow; it's probably the most widely quoted, and in a lot of people's minds it represents the market.

Participation Rate:

If your contract has a participation rate of say, 75%, it means you will get interest paid into your contract equal to 75% of the growth of the Dow for the time period selected. So if the Dow goes up 10% you will get 7.5%; it's pretty simple.

Some contracts will have a 100% participation rate but impose an "administrative fee" or "spread." This is just another way of making it work. Let's say that your contract has a "spread" of 2.5%. If the Dow goes up 10%, then they would deduct the 2.5% from that number to get to your interest amount, which in this case would then be 7.5%.

In the two examples I have used, the resulting interest credit to you is the same, but the two ways of calculating the rate of interest will be a lot different if the market goes up 20%

If the Dow goes up 20% and you have a 75% "participation" rate you will be credited 15% (75% of 20%).

If the Dow goes up 20% and you have a participation rate of 100% with a "spread" of 2.5%, you will get credited 17.5% (100% - 2.5%). That's a big difference.
On the other hand, if the Dow goes up only 6% and your contract has a participation rate of 75%, you will get 4.5%. But if the Dow goes up only 6% and your 100% participation contract has a spread of 2.5%, then you would get only 3.5%.

Note: Usually the company can reset the rates each year as market conditions change, because the company has to go buy options that make this happen at what might be very different prices.

How to Choose?

That's pretty simple, but a question you might have is: **How does a reasonable person choose which index when <u>no one knows what the market will do?</u>** Chapter 6 covers that question and gives you a plan.

There are a few more details that go into determining the amount of interest that you earn. For instance, some contracts have "caps." These are upside limits on how much interest you can earn. In Chapter 2 I shared with you how these things are designed. Part of the design might be to put in an upside cap on the total return the contract can have in any one year. This is part of the trade off in which you get protection against market declines.

So for example, if your contract has a "cap" of 12%, then the most you can earn is 12%, even if the market goes up more.

Now let's talk about how the gain in the index is measured. We will continue using the Dow as an example. This involves a lot of jargon and more details than most people investing in Index Annuities need to know, but in case you have a special need or simply want to play the game a little harder than most, I am including this information.

The contract date when your annuity is issued starts the clock ticking. So you will get extra interest one year later if the Dow is higher, based upon your participation rate or spread, minimum crediting (floor), and caps. That's makes perfect sense and that simple method is called "point to point annual method."

It's called "point to point" because the index is measured off of two points, the starting one and the ending one, and "annual" because these two points are one year apart. A lot of people use this method and I bet you will too.

There are other methods that the companies have come up with to entice the analytical people to invest. Engineers, lawyers, accountants and math people love these types of investments because they can use all of these options.

Averaging

You can choose options that calculate the return on a daily or monthly average, called averaging. Many times the averaging method puts a cap on any particular "up" day, but no floor on the "down" days.

Point to Point Over a Period Other Than a Year

Above we discussed the easiest to understand and the most popular option, which was point to point annual. Some companies offer point to point over several years or even over the life of the contract. These would appropriately have different caps, spreads and participation rates. So if you think the Dow is really cheap, but don't want to lose any money and feel that it will be a lot higher in 5 years, and the different participation rates for a 5 year point to point will make you more money than annual point to point, you might choose a company with a contract and option for this method.

High Water Mark Method

Using the high water mark method you are credited interest based on the highest your chosen index goes during the term of the contract (or other period that's offered).

While this seems like a great selection, you might do better -if the market goes up one year then back down, then back up and so forth- with an annual point to point method, as you can earn the same dollar multiple times. This is because you don't give back any market declines once credited to the contract.

Low Water Mark

The low water mark method will use the lowest index value during the term of the contract (or other period as offered) as the beginning value. It's an attractive idea, but there will be other offsets. There is no free lunch, but there are times when you may select this entree from the buffet- perhaps when the markets seem in great turmoil and when the other factors, such as caps and spreads, don't seem to change much when you choose it.

Fixed Rate with Equity Participation

Look for two different ways they do this. The first version puts a part of the money in a fixed interest account, say 5%, and the rest is put into an annual reset method. The second version credits the money a fixed rate plus a portion of the index's gain (but no loss). This results in a smoother overall rate of return; earning nothing is impossible, but earning a lot is hard to do. This type of method takes a conservative investment and makes it even more so. I find it rare that people choose this, as the main point of Index Annuities is avoiding the declines in the markets.

Bond Indexed

The bond indexed method credits interest to your contract based off of the index representing the return from owning a portfolio of bonds. So, instead of wanting the S&P500 to go up in value, you will want the bond index (usually measured by what was known as the Lehman Brothers Bond Index, now called Barclays Cap Bond Index) to go up. Generally that index will turn in its best returns when the interest rates that bonds pay are going down, because that causes the values of the existing bonds, and hence the index, to go up.

Why use an Index Annuity to invest in Bonds?

"Why would someone want this?" you might ask. Wouldn't it perhaps be better to just buy the bonds themselves? Well, if you buy the bonds you don't get the ability to defer interest and perhaps avoid creditors, which might be an important factor.

More likely the biggest reason people choose an Index Annuity with bond indexing is that they think bond prices may go <u>up</u> in the future.

However, if you own treasuries and rates go up, your bonds will go <u>down</u> in value, perhaps significantly. Using an Index Annuity that pays you interest based on the change in value of the bond index, this option will protect you from this market value decline. Pretty cool!

Just like with Stock based indexes the Bond index allows you to get interest credited to your account based on increases in the index but not have interest that has been credited to your account taken away if the index (either bond or stocks based index) declines.

Chapter 6

The Process of Choosing an Index

If you KNEW which index and method would work out best you would use that knowledge to make a lot of money owning more aggressive securities. If you knew what was going to happen in the future you would not need or want the safety that Index Annuities offer.

What, you don't know the future?

But you don't know the future, none of us do, and that is why you are reading this. Maybe like most people you are concerned about the future and don't want to lose any more money, or you want to earn more on your CDs but more than that, <u>I bet that you want to know the best way to get the maximum income off of your investments for your retirement!</u>

In the next chapter, I will give you a list of a few of the most commonly used indexes. But first I want to discuss the index selection process in general. Probably what is important to you is one of the following:

1) The guaranteed minimum interest rates in the contract and how they might be more than what your CDs are paying, or…

2) The guarantee of a great income, backed by a colossal insurance company, that will be guaranteed for as long as you live. (Isn't that what retirement is all about, income and cash flow?)

What to do?

Index Annuities are all about safety, certainty, lowering risk, and guaranteed values, as well as perhaps an income for your retirement. The insurance companies have produced quite an array of options you can use to make your annuity perform based on your requirements. You or your advisor will have to choose which indexes you will tie your interest to, and your contract will be based on the growth of the index you choose. That index measures the growth in the stock market; if the index loses value in any given period your index annuity will not, so this is a "heads you win, tails you break even" way of trying to get the great returns of the stock market.

Since no one knows what will happen in the stock market in the next year, it's probably a good idea to use broad indexes that cover the entire market, unless you want to base your interest growth on only one sector of the market. If you have a strong feeling about a certain sector of the market, go for it. For example, if you are sure the overseas markets are going to soar next year, you might choose the EAFE index as the one that will determine how much interest you will be paid.

Be cautious: The reason people invest in Index Annuities instead of other types of securities, stocks or even variable annuities is because they have matured to a point, perhaps through wisdom or perhaps through experience where they want *guarantees* instead of great *gains*. So if you have matured to a point where the conclusion is more important that being right on a segment of the market, then you will probably choose a more well-rounded index.

Diversify!

I suggest that it might be in your best interest to choose several different indexes (sometimes in the same contract, or you might need several different contracts), and use the annual point to point method (see Chapter 5). Many times the company will offer you the ability to pick several different indexes and let you choose different indexes for different portions of the money. Furthermore, they may allow you to choose their own combination of indexes which may be an average of two of the indexes.

For example, you may be able to put 25% into each of 4 different indexes, or the company may offer a selection which represents 25% of the money being in each of 4 different indexes. It will be easier to understand what they are offering when you know a little about the underlying indexes. I will get to that in the next chapter.

Multiple Contracts

We talked about diversifying, and you can do that either by choosing multiple indexes within one contract, or by choosing multiple contracts. Here are some reasons why you might decide it's best to choose multiple contracts, rather than simply choose multiple indexes within one contract:

Reasons to buy more than one Index Annuity contract:

- You want to diversify your risk between insurance companies.

- You want to diversify your risk between contracts at the same company.

- You want to save money that you might spend on riders by buying them on some contracts but not others.

- You want to get maximum usage of the extra death benefit riders, and that means buying different contracts to "insure" different people.

- You want to make your estate plan simple and have a separate contract on each beneficiary; this is especially handy if you want to stretch an IRA.

- You want to get junior members of the family interested in managing money, and having different members "help" you manage a different contract is helpful.

- You want different ownership registration. For example, you have one that is an IRA, and another that is not.

- You may want to collateralize part of a contract (it can be done) but don't want to tie up all of your contracts with the same agreement.

- You want to break up the ownership of the assets for estate planning.

- The most common: You want to buy different indexes and use different crediting methods with the money.

- You want to keep some of the money a secret from your spouse (not a joke!)

Chapter 7

A List of Common Indexes

In previous chapters we have talked about the fact that an Index Annuity is tied to a particular index (or group of indexes), and the performance of that index is used to determine the interest that is paid. We have also talked about the process of selecting an index or group of indexes.

Perhaps you want to focus on small caps, or large cap stocks. Maybe you want to focus on domestic stocks or overseas stocks. In this chapter I have provided a brief listing of some of the most common indexes used for Index Annuities, along with a brief description of each. There are others, and if you are interested in one that is not listed here, or would like to consider a larger list, please talk to your agent or financial advisor.

Dow Jones 30 Industrials
(USA large companies)

http://www.nyse.com/

This index is also called simply "the Dow" or "the Dow 30." It is the most famous of all indexes, and tracks on a capitalization weighted* basis the changes in the stock prices of 30 of the largest industrial companies traded in the USA. This index is price weighted as opposed to most others which are market weighted. Price weighted means that the price of the stock and its changes are what changes the index, rather than the change in the total market value of the company. Please refer to the discussion of market capitalization weighted indexes further down. While the Dow is one of the well-quoted indexes, it is composed of only 30 of the largest companies in America.

The FTSE 100 Index

http://www.ftse.com

A London-based index, the FTSE 100 is also known as the "footsie," and is a capitalization weighted* index of the largest 100 stocks on the London Stock Exchange. It represents a lot of economic activity around the world, both inside and outside of the USA.

MSCI EAFE
(foreign stocks)

http://www.mscibarra.com

This index is a market capitalization weighted* index of stocks from about 21 different countries. It is the oldest index tracking foreign (from a US investor's point of view) stocks. Its EAFE initials stand for Europe Australia and the Far East. It is maintained by Morgan Stanley Capital International, whose website is above.

NASDAQ Composite
(over the counter stocks)

http://www.nasdaq.com/

This index is one that tracks all the securities listed on the NASDAQ stock market, which currently includes over 3000 names. The NASDAQ has a history of being attractive to smaller companies, although many very large ones are listed there, and of being more sensitive to technology stocks. The stocks in the index include both US and non-US companies. The NASDAQ is capitalization weighted.*

NASDAQ 100
(100 largest non-financial NASDAQ companies)

http://www.nasdaq.com/

This index is a market capitalization weighted index* of only the top 100 non-financial companies listed on the NASDAQ. They can be US companies or foreign, but not financial companies (banks, brokerages or investment companies like closed end funds.)

Standard and Poor's (S&P) 500

www.standardandpoors.com

The Standard and Poor's 500 index is probably one of the most followed and quoted indexes here in the US. It is probably second only to the Dow Jones 30 industrials. When you hear how the stock market performed on any given day, the newscasters are probably quoting, in part, this index.

It is market capitalization weighted* and composed of the 500 largest companies as listed in America, with only a few exceptions. It is considered a good measure of the growth or decline of stocks in America.

Standard and Poor's (S&P) 100

www.standardandpoors.com

This index is made up of 100 of the largest companies in the Standard and Poor's 500. To be included in this index, options need to be traded on the underlying security. It is designed to be a diverse representation of the large companies generally in the USA. It is market capitalization weighted.

Russell 2000

www.russell.com/Indexes

This market capitalization weighted* index is comprised of 200 primarily US stocks that have total market values of generally under $1 billion each. These are referred to as small capitalization or "small cap" stocks. These stocks and this index tend to move faster with changing economic trends than do the indexes of larger securities.

The Lehman Aggregate Bond Index
(This tracks <u>bonds, not stocks,</u> and is soon to be renamed after its new owner, Barclays Capital.)

The Lehman Aggregate Bond Index is a market capitalization weighted index of bonds (<u>not stocks</u> like the other indexes mentioned above). The bonds include good quality corporate bonds and government bonds, including mortgage-backed securities, but does not include municipals or treasury inflation protected securities. This index tracks the changes in values, and hence interest rates, on fixed income securities traded in the US.

* What does "Market Capitalization Weighted" mean?

Most indexes are computed this way. In a "Market Capitalization Weighted," or a value weighted index (same thing), the index changes how much weight each stock has in it based upon that stock's total market capitalization. This means that the higher the total value of the company in the market, the more it counts in the index.

For example if Microsoft, being one of the most valuable overall companies in America today, goes up or down 10% in price, it would make a much bigger difference in the index than say, General Motors would when it goes up or down 10%. The total value of a company is based upon the number of shares outstanding and the market value of the company, and since General Motors' total value is a lot lower than Microsoft's, its movements in the market count a lot less.

The math supporting these changes is changed daily, so as a stock moves up or down in total value, that change matters increasingly more so in the index.

This is both good and bad. It is good in that when a whole group of stocks are growing a lot in value in the market place (such as when the technology stocks in the late 1990's went up a lot in total value), they make up a bigger percentage of the index. So the more they go up, the more they count in the index. On the downside, the same is true when a company or industry is shrinking in total market value; it will count less and less in the index.

Market capitalization weighted indexes are good for Index Annuities, as they tend to generate momentum-driven upswings. That's great when you're getting paid interest based upon growth, but in years when people who own index funds are getting the brunt of the downside your money is safe. It may not grow, but as we have discussed, it will not go down because some index goes negative for the year.

Chapter 8

What Guarantees All of These Benefits?

You get to pick the answer to this question.

There are many insurance companies in this business and more are coming onboard all the time. Find one that you feel comfortable with and have your agent check out their contracts to see if they fit your needs.

I suggest the following:

- Choose a large company. They will have the resources and economies of scale that make the business profitable for them and you and hence, will keep your contract more competitive, as the business is getting better all the time.

- It should be a name you know or that you can check out easily.

- It should have great ratings from the rating agencies. See the Appendix for a list of Independent Rating Agencies.

- It should have a serious stake in the Index Annuity business. Even if it is a large company, you probably don't want a company that is only sticking its toe into the Index Annuity market; I suggest that you want to see some commitment.

State Guarantee Associations

Beyond doing your own research to find a company you are comfortable with, realize that insurance companies are licensed, supervised and regulated by the state governments of each of the states in which they do business.

When a state insurance commissioner determines that an insurance company is insolvent, the state will usually work hard to get them taken over by another insurance company, which will then assume responsibility for the products, claims and liabilities of the previous company. Failing that, should the company be forced to liquidate, the various state guaranty associations are activated.

When there is a shortage of money to meet the obligations of the policyholders of the company in trouble, the other insurance companies licensed in that state are assessed, and required to pay, a share of the amount required to meet the claims of resident policyholders. That is fascinating and very wise, in that all these fiercely competitive companies are forced to pony up to fund each other's losses should one fail.

Each state works basically the same way in order to protect its citizens.

In 1983 the states created the National Organization of Life and Health Insurance Guaranty Associations (www.nolhga.com). If the failed company does business in more than two states, NOLHGA coordinates the development of a plan to protect policyholders.

This is a pretty good system and has withstood the test of time.

Chapter 9

What Expenses Do I Have to Pay?

Costs and fees do not matter in Index Annuities like they do in other investment vechiles or variable annuities. Securities of all kinds (even index funds) have fees and costs associated with them. They include:

- Management fees for the investment managers
- Administrative fees
- Legal fees
- Trading and research costs
- Spreads that result from trading

The good news is that your Index Annuity charges none of those fees to you. This is because you elect to earn interest based upon the performance of an index; if it goes up, you get your share, and if it doesn't, you either get nothing or whatever the contract says you will get in that situation. It may give you a little interest even if the index you select goes down.

There are no variable returns or superstar managers with private jets. There are no egos to feed or advertising to do to advertise fund returns. There is no board of directors for whom you need to pay expenses. You get a net number, period. Because you are given a net number based upon the performance of a published index, you are not subject to the host of expenses and conflicts of interests that come with other investments.

Also, because it's not part of the deal, you also don't get the every-once-in-a-while huge upside that those other investments can deliver. With an Index Annuity you get no market downside, expenses you elect, and a lot more certainty.

Riders

Now, should you elect to get certain riders, notably the income type rider I have referred to in Chapter 3, you will be charged for that rider. That is an expense, and an associated benefit, that you consciously <u>elect</u> and <u>volunteer to pay for</u>.

The cost of the riders is pretty consistent but some companies do change the cost from time to time. I have included in the "questions to ask your agent" section in the back a question about which riders can change in price and which cannot.

Cost-free Benefits

While the additional riders that you might choose each carry an additional cost, there <u>are</u> some benefits of annuities in general that carry <u>no</u> extra cost to you or the company:

<u>Income tax deferral</u> in an annuity is granted via the Internal Revenue Code. Your income taxes have paid for that benefit, so you might as well take advantage of it.

The <u>exemption from creditor attacks</u> is given to you (or not) by your state's laws. Ask a lawyer what the status is in your state.

The other benefits and riders which are part of the package, and the costs and trade-offs, are what make Index Annuities work for you and be profitable for the insurance company too. Both are important.

Chapter 10

The End Game:

Withdrawing Capital and Profits
Surrender Penalties
Income Taxes

Withdrawing Capital and Profits

There are a number of ways of accessing your money. Most people will simply call their agent or the company when they need the money and get a check in the mail.

Most companies offer a free-of-penalty 10% free withdrawal once a year. Further, they might offer other options to avoid any surrender charge if you are confined at home or in a hospital or a nursing home. Any required minimum distributions (for IRA accounts) might be free of penalties as well.

Depending on your company and contract, you might have an 'income rider' to allow you to have access to an amount of money that is considerably above what the contract may be worth. I have mentioned this several times. There is a form that usually needs to be completed and submitted to the company. It sounds easy getting the money, because it is.

However if the income rider isn't going to be used and you want a fixed program, the companies usually offer a variety of them. These include:

- Interest only- You can ask the company to send you the interest (the gain in the index that you earn each year.

- Installments for a guaranteed period- You can choose to receive equal installments for a period of time you select. They would all be equal and the contract would not change after the payments started, although they would include an interest component based upon an interest rate, not upon the stock market.

- Installments for Life- These payments would be fixed at the beginning and never change for the remainder of your life.

- Installments for life but with a guaranteed period- These payments would be fixed and continue for the rest of your life, but if you died before a specified number of years, they would continue for that number of years. For example, it might be life with a 20 year period certain; if you took this option and died in year 10, the payments would continue to be paid to your beneficiary for another 10 years (for a total of 20 years).

- Installments for a specified amount- You can tell the company to send you a certain sum of money and they will until it's gone; then the payments stop. No guarantees. Usually the contract continues to function and earn interest based upon its indexes with this option.

- Joint and Survivor- You can have equal payments until your death, then have a percentage of those go to your survivor. It might be 100% or 50% or some other figure. The choice of how much goes to your survivor, of course, as well as both of your ages, determines the size of the payments.

What most people will do…

Most people will skip all the fancy stuff and ask the company to send them the guaranteed income on the first day of each contract year, or let it compound while they live off of other sources of income, saving this income for a rainy day or to leave to their children or charity.

Surrender Penalties

Index Annuity contracts carry a surrender charge to give the insurance company the time to let all the pieces work. If you buy the contract and want your money back three months later, the company is out all the costs and has no time for the bond to work or for the call to appreciate and earn your return. It would be unfair to the other policyholders and to the company to let you out of the contract at that point, so there are surrender penalties to make it all work out equally.

The amount and timing of surrender penalties is added into the mix so that it all works and the insurance company is protected, and that makes your money safe too. So when you are looking at different contracts and see different surrender penalties, know in theory that they are there for a reason- to protect you as a policy holder from other people hurting the company by pulling their money out early.

Given all of the math that goes into making Index Annuities so simple, also be aware that it is a very competitive marketplace. It's not like the old days when only a couple of companies offered these products. I am comforted by that and it's a big reason why I think this idea is ready for the challenges that our generation is prepared to give to it.

Nobody likes surrender penalties. Why does a bank need to charge you to take your own money out of a CD early, or the government when you take your money out of your IRA prior to age 59 ½?

The reasons they exist are to protect the institution from losing money, either because people change their minds or, in the case of banks, interest rates change a lot.

For a bank CD, if you have a 3% rate for 4 years and rates went to 4% and there was no surrender penalty, then you would cancel the 3% and get them to pay you 4%- that will cost the bank an extra $1000 a year on a $100,000 CD. But the reverse is not true; if rates go to 2% you will not surrender your CD and let the pay you $1000 less. Given this, the bank could lose a lot of money if there were no surrender penalties.

So in order to protect the banking system, the system allows them to charge a penalty on early withdrawal. It is basically the same way with a lot of financial products, including, Index Annuities.

If the penalties didn't exist then the insurance companies might be in a position to lose money and thus put other investors at risk. Perhaps it's best to think of the surrender penalty as a way of keeping that other guy from hurting you!

For Index Annuities the surrender penalties play an even more important role. Keep in mind that the insurance company needs to:
- Buy the zero coupon bonds that mature at the end of the term of the contract, and
- Buy calls that generate the returns, and

- Cover the costs to issue them and service the business (including the commissions to your agent)

Since they don't know what the cost or value of these things will be at any given time during the life of the contract, they need a surrender charge to make sure they can't lose too much money. They might lose some anyway, but the surrender charge keeps those "other people" from jumping ship, and this makes it safer for all investors. The size and length of the penalty (they usually decrease quickly over time) allows the company to buy longer term bonds, and thereby gives them the ability to offer you greater participation rates and other terms.

Usually there are a few exceptions to the surrender penalties; however, not all contracts offer all of these exceptions, and some might offer others not listed:

- They let you take 10% of your money out each year with no penalty; try doing that at your bank or with the IRS!

- If you are confined to a nursing home or hospital they waive the penalty or give you an easy out.*

- If you need to take the money out due to a required minimum distribution (RMD) because it's IRA money.

- If you die, frequently the penalty is waived or your heirs are given a good way of getting access to the money.
- Many companies have deals for you if you need the money back, payment programs over short

time periods, or other offers that can reduce their risk and get your money back to you.

In any event, the surrender penalty is built into the math that makes it all work. Please be sure you understand any penalties included in your contract.

The marketplace for Index Annuities is very competitive and is getting more so. Furthermore, your state must pass judgment on each contract before it is allowed to be shown to you, so you have a couple of things protecting you, apart from your own good sense.

If your contract has a bonus feature, usually the penalty is in addition to recapturing part or all of the bonus. If you are given a 10% bonus and the contract has a 10% penalty, don't think they offset each other; that wouldn't make sense, would it? The company will take back the bonus and charge you a penalty as well. Of course, the good news is that both the "take backs" decline in most years, so you usually end up keeping the 10% bonus, and the penalty is a lot less than a couple of bad days in the stock market.

Enjoy the bonus and the benefits, and avoid the penalties by either leaving the money in for the full term and letting it work for you, or by working with one of the exceptions!

A last word… before you pay a penalty see if the company has a loan option that may help you get through until the end of the penalty period. So if you need money that may be a way to get it at a lot lower cost.

*Index Annuities and Health Care Expenses

What about <u>hospital care</u> and <u>nursing home expenses</u>? Annuities, especially Index Annuities, are not home health care or nursing home insurance policies, but they usually offer a lot of help in the process of paying for home health care, hospital stays, and nursing homes.

Index Annuities offer a lot of assistance with these expenses by <u>not going down in value</u> when the market declines. That can be very helpful, as few things could hurt more than to sell your assets at bargain prices to pay for a nursing home or home health care episode.

Also, most of the contracts have riders of one sort or another that will waive the surrender penalty, if it's still in effect, should the owner check into a nursing home or assisted living facility. If this is likely for you, check the rider to make sure that the ownership is set up correctly for the person who is likely to need the money for such expenses.

Further, in many states annuities are exempt from claims from creditors, which means if there is some catastrophic episode and the medical bills far outweigh your ability to pay, that protection usually afforded only to insurance contracts (life , variable and fixed annuities) might save the day!

Paying Income Taxes on the Profits

Let's talk about taxation of this interest. Annuities are tax deferred, not tax free. If you are a natural person (not a corporation or partnership) person, the interest is not taxed until it is withdrawn. With an annuity you have the ability to withdraw money as you need it and minimize the taxes; after all, why pay taxes on income you don't need?

The interest can remain in the annuity and be compounded, and perhaps you can time your withdrawals so as to reduce your overall income taxes. For example, you might choose to offset that income against high medical costs one year, or take income one year and not another to avoid paying tax on your social security income.

Perhaps you live in a high tax state but are planning a move to Florida (no state income tax); you might choose to leave the money in until you get to Florida to skip paying state income taxes on it. See your tax advisor for more information on this.

Also, if you are hovering around that income level that results in you paying tax on your social security you might, with your accountant's help, be able to take the income out in such a way as to avoid paying taxes on your social security.

When you pass away and leave the annuity to your family they will pay the income tax when they take the money out. This might be good if they are in a lower income tax bracket than you are, or if you spread it out among a host of people.

State and local income taxes play a role in planning for annuities like this, especially if you are planning to move to a low or no tax state when you retire, as it makes little sense to pay local taxes on money you are saving for retirement. Annuities usually make a lot of sense and might allow you to avoid those local taxes altogether.

On the other hand, be aware of possibly deferring the taxes for too long. If your tax bracket is lower than your children's (for example, if you live in Florida and they live in New York City), and the money and associated tax liability will likely go to them, then you might want to consider withdrawing your interest while you can. This is not a negative on the Index Annuity; it still probably makes sense, but it means that deferring the taxes too long should be avoided.

<u>Keep in mind that</u> taxable income is a whole lot better to have than capital losses! Furthermore, this taxable income can be managed and timed to make it do the best work for you!

Chapter 11

What Should I Expect from My Agent?

Your best ally is your agent. Your agent is doing this type of work everyday and has probably faced every question and issue you have, or he has thought of it before. He should be there to assist you when the time comes to get income out or deal with riders and so forth. Stay in touch with him or her.

You should reasonably expect your agent to:

- Understand who you are and what your needs are, as well as understand your capacity to handle risk.

- Find an appropriate company and product that suits your needs and desires.

- Explain that Index Annuity to you. See questions in the following checklist to go over with your agent, so that you understand what you are buying and the benefits, riders and surrender penalties that accompany it.

- Process your transaction on a timely basis, keeping you in the know as to how it's progressing.

- Be available to handle questions about your investment as time passes, and recommend and explain the most appropriate simplest way of looking toward what you want or need to do, at the least cost, considering penalties, loss of growth, income taxes etc.

- If things change, (the law, the company, the contract, the markets or the indexes) keep you informed and make

appropriate recommendations that are in your best
interest.

A Checklist:
BEFORE you invest, review this important list!

Here is a handy checklist of things you will want to discuss
with your agent and consider for yourself before you invest. I
suggest that you tear it out and go over it one by one with your
agent. He or she should be very happy to do it, as it means you
will understand what you are investing in.

There are no "right" or "wrong" answers, it's only important
that you understand what you have! There are many variations
of contracts; the point of this is to have a good understanding of
what you are offered and make a decision based on what the
truth is.

It's funny in a way- a other securities' prospectus have 100's of
pages of long legal words to tell you about the risks of loss, the
risk of currency translations, the management fees, the costs to
acquire and dispose of the investment, as well as the rather
large annual costs to run the show. A variable annuity has the
same and more. Yet these few questions cover most, if not all,
of the details, costs and risks that are involved with an Index
Annuity. You might be comforted by this element of
simplicity.

In writing this I thought about the questions I would want to
know to ask if my own mother was investing in an Index
Annuity, so maybe I have covered the same area twice, but
that's OK. To understand sometimes requires looking at things
from different angles. If you would like a print out of these

questions (They will be updated as we get more input.) go to: http://www.alakazampublishing.com/FIA

Questions to go over with your agent:

Note: In these questions, when I refer to the "markets" I mean the indexes and method you have chosen.

[] Will this investment be helped by a person or a trust? (This is important as the tax law does not allow corporations or non-natural persons to get these benefits!)

[] What happens to my ability to draw an income stream even if the markets don't go up?

[] What happens to my account value if the markets don't go up in value and I draw an income stream from it anyway?

[] If the markets don't go up and I draw the income stream from it, what happens when the account value is gone? Can I continue to get an income check, and for how long? (This is the "sleep at night" question!)

[] If the market goes up, how much of that gain will show as profit (interest) for me?

[] If I think the stock market is going down what can I do to make money? Is there a fixed or bond account I can tie my gains to instead of the stock market?

[] How often can I change the index and method that is used to compute my gains?

[] What are the charges for any riders that will be on the contract?

[] Is there a minimum profit (interest credit) in the contract regardless of what the index does?

[] If I surrender the contract before the end of the surrender penalty period, what happens?

[] How financially strong is the company that issues the contract?

[] Does my state have any money set aside to help me if the company fails?

[] Is this investment FDIC insured?

[] What is guaranteed in the contract and what is not?

[] Does this contract have a guaranteed income feature or rider like the type mentioned in this book?

[] Is my money guaranteed to be safe from market losses no matter what?

[] Are the costs of the riders that I have chosen guaranteed?

[] Which riders that I have chosen can be cancelled, and what occurs to their benefits if I decide to cancel?

[] When I do access money from the policy, how does that change things such as income riders, crediting of interest, etc.?

[] If I am investing with IRA or 403(b) or other pretax money, will the required minimum distributions (RMDs) change any of the guarantees or benefits under the contract?

[] If I am investing in a contract with a minimum floor, also called a minimum interest rate, how is that paid? Each year? Or perhaps over the life of the contract? If it is my intent to live off of that, how will taking it out change things?

[] Explain how the nursing home or home health care riders work, if included?

[] Confirm that each year that any interest earned cannot be lost in later years due to market declines.
[] Explain when I can start getting cash flow and more, when is it in my best interest to get cash flow from the contract?

[] Have I set up the ownership of the contract and the beneficiaries in a way that makes my desires likely to be fulfilled? (i.e. estate planning, creditor protection, income tax, social security taxation planning)

[] Would I be better off having multiple contracts with the same amount of total money?

[] Will you, Mr. Agent, be available to help me each year to decide how to handle the renewal and the selection of index and methods?

[] If I have an income rider on the contract, how will it be affected if I take distributions or die?

[] If I am the owner or annuitant and I pass away, are the surrender penalties waived?

[] If I have and exercise an income rider, when I pass away will any unused income credits benefit my spouse or family? What will they get?

Questions for <u>you</u>:

[] With the investment in this contract, are you diversified enough to feel comfortable? Please be reasonable and responsible when making any investment, and don't put all your money in any one place, no matter how attractive it is.

[] Has the agent asked you to write a check to him/her instead of the company? If yes, cancel that check and report them to the authorities.

[] Are you being forced or coerced into this transaction? If yes, take some time to consider the investment, so you don't feel rushed.

[] Will the timing of the cash flow from this investment and your other cash flows work together to give you what you need?

[] If you normally discuss such things with your children, have you done so in this case?

Chapter 12

Want to Get the Benefit of Indexing but Without Investing in an Annuity?

You don't have to buy an annuity to protect your money from market declines, but know that:

Index <u>Mutual Funds</u> Offer <u>NO</u> Guarantee

Index funds do NOT offer any guarantee that they won't go down due to market declines; in fact, they track the index up or down, so if you want to avoid the downside, Index Mutual Funds are not for you. If you can get it right though, and catch the index fund just as the markets are about to take a big run upward, and further, sell at or near the top, you will be lucky indeed. Of course, if you can do that you belong on Wall Street making the big dollars! <u>If you want to take that kind of risk in your life (betting that you can time the markets just right)</u>, you do not belong in an Index Annuity, CD or Structured Product.

Equity Linked Certificates of Deposit (CDs)

Many banks offer equity linked CDs. They have much the same design as the annuity does except they tend to be short term, usually a year or 18 months. <u>CDs lack a number of the advantages of Index Annuities</u>, such as:

- Tax deferral- Usually you must pay tax on the interest while you own the CD (a 6% rate is typical, so instead of saving money by deferring taxes you are paying up front.

- <u>No income guarantees</u>- If the markets do nothing, you get nothing. But as I discussed earlier, with Index Annuities if the markets do nothing over the term of the index annuity and your contract has the proper design or rider, then at least you end up with a lifetime income guarantee, even if it has to come out of the insurance company's pocket. With an Indexed CD you get the market moves over a usually short time and that's that.

- No creditor protection as an Index Annuity might provide if your state allows.

- A limited amount of insurance- The FDIC has limits on the amount of deposits they insure; any amount of money in the CD above that amount would not be insured. There is no such limit with Index Annuities. While they are not backed by the FDIC, they are backed by an insurance company that you will approve of, and such companies have no limit on their guarantees. (Note: If the company will issue the contract, they do usually want to be notified if you are going to put in more than $1 million.)

- No bonus features- Many Index Annuities offer a bonus feature for signing up. Banks generally do not offer that. Heck- banks don't even give away toasters anymore!

- While the CDs are likely to be shorter term in nature and the need for exception to the penalties on the CD is less important, they generally do not offer any exception for nursing home or medical expenses.

In short banks, through CDs, do offer index products, but while they protect your principal, they miss a lot of the features of Index Annuities, including the one I like the most- income guarantees.

Structured Products

A structured product is usually **corporate note or preferred stock** which is supported by the zero coupon bond and call options like Index Annuities are designed to be.

It promises to pay interest like the CD and the Index Annuity, based upon the change in value of the index. These can work well and are backed by the entire institution and usually carry the credit rating of the issuing bank or institution. Like an Index CD though, it lacks most of the real advantages that I think someone looking at an Index Annuity would want, such as:

- Tax Deferral- Usually with those structured products you pay tax while you wait to see what you make (a 6% rate is typical), so instead of saving money by deferring taxes, you are paying up front.

- Income guarantees- So if the markets do nothing, you get nothing. As I discussed previously, if the markets do nothing over the term of the index annuity and your contract has the proper design or rider, then at least you end up with a lifetime income guarantee, even if it has to come out of the insurance company's pocket. With a structured product you get the market moves over a usually short time and that's that.

- Creditor protection- as an Index Annuity might provide if your state allows.

- Bonus features- Many Index Annuities offer a bonus feature for signing up. Structured products do not offer that.

- Typically, structured products do not offer any early redemption features. If you want out, they will give you a price and it's a 'take it or leave it' situation. Index Annuities, tell you in advance what the value of your investment would be (as a minimum), should you desire to get out of the contract early.

Chapter 13

Summary

For the vast majority of people this is maybe a 'no brainer' to use with at least a portion of their retirement dollars.

With the recent market crashes and layoffs, nearly everyone is worried and even angry about the lack of supervision on Wall Street and in our financial institutions, yet for all of us retirement is either here or getting so close that we can see the whites of its eyes.

Enter the Indexed Annuity… no more management fees and costs, no more capital gains distribution, no more market losses, fewer sleepless nights, and no fear of turning on the news to hear the fear and worry being injected into us by the media.

Index Annuities may help ease many of the problems of the day, and of this generation, with their four-part punch:

1) Participation in market gains but no more market losses, your value backed up by your insurance company
2) Deferral of income taxes until you retire to a lower bracket
3) Lower costs and expenses
4) Guaranteed income based on an amount that may potentially be far in excess of what you put in

Again, theses features may differ between different contracts and are based upon the options and rider selected.

These are not perfect investments; it would be nice if all of this could be done in a money market fund with no commitment on anyone's part, but that's not possible, just as it's not possible to own a home without going to closing and dealing with the details. Over time though, I believe both will prove to be smart decisions.

For most people, who have been financially disappointed in the recent markets and who, are looking at some potentially scary things on the horizon that could last a long time, such as budget deficits and de-leveraging, I just can't imagine a better alternative.

We get guaranteed interest rates above what CDs and government bonds are paying, and capture some market upside when that happens, but no downside.

How Do I Get More Information?

Ask your agent for more information. If you don't have an agent, log onto http://www.alakazampublishing.com/FIA for more information; generally the insurance companies are a poor source of information, until you become a policyholder.

Glossary

Annuity- Fixed – A contract between an insurance company and usually an individual, which pays either a fixed interest rate or fixed participation in an index.

Annuity-Variable – an investment security contract offered by an insurance company, aptly described as a mutual fund within a tax-deferred wrapper.

Annuity- Deferred – The internal revenue code allows both types of annuities (fixed and variable) if held by a natural person to defer the income taxation of the gains or interest credited to the contract until it is taken out.

Cap – a rate of interest which is the highest rate that an Index Annuity can pay in that time period. If you are using an annual point to point method with a cap of 10%, the most you can earn is 10% in any year, even it the index you have chosen goes up 12%.

Index Annuity - A fixed annuity which accrues interest at a rate based upon the appreciation but not the depreciation of a well known index between points in time.

Index Certificate of Deposit – A CD that accrues interest at a rate based upon the appreciation but not the depreciation of a well known index between points in time.

Market Value Adjustment - a change in the net proceeds from the early redemption of an annuity from its account value, due to the appreciation or depreciation of the markets (generally the bond markets

Minimum Guarantee (benefit of an Index Annuity) – A minimum positive interest rate that will be earned and credited, regardless of the performance of the underlying index.

Spread –a number representing percentage points that are taken off the index to determine how much interest you earn in any given period. If you have a spread of 2.5% and the index and method you have chosen earns 15%, your contract will be credited with 12.5% interest for the year. The spread cannot make you earn negative interest; for example, if the index earns 1.5% for the year and you have a 2.5% spread you would earn nothing for the year.

Surrender Penalties or Charges – used by the insurance company to protect itself and thereby you as a contract holder, and recover costs if an annuity is cashed in early. See Chapter 10.

Appendix:

Independent Rating Agencies

There are several companies that provide quality ratings on insurance companies:

A.M. Best Company (www.ambest.com)

The Fitch Ratings Insurance Group (www.fitchibca.com)

Moody's (www.moodys.com)

Standard & Poor's (www.sandp.com)

www.ingramcontent.com/pod-product-compliance
Lightning Source LLC
Chambersburg PA
CBHW061835220326
41599CB00027B/5294